Mezzo-Soprano/Belter

THE SINGER'S ANTHOLOGY OF GERSHWIN SONGS

A collection of Gershwin songs, curated for today's singer, transposed into appropriate keys, based on original sources.

Edited by Richard Walters

GERSHWIN® and GEORGE GERSHWIN® are registered trademarks of Gershwin Enterprises
IRA GERSHWIN™ is a trademark of Gershwin Enterprises
PORGY AND BESS® is a registered trademark of Porgy and Bess Enterprises

ISBN 978-1-5400-2261-5

HAL•LEONARD®

Visit Hal Leonard Online at
www.halleonard.com

Contact Us:
Hal Leonard
7777 West Bluemound Road
Milwaukee, WI 53213
Email: info@halleonard.com

In Europe contact:
Hal Leonard Europe Limited
Distribution Centre, Newmarket Road
Bury St Edmunds, Suffolk, IP33 3YB
Email: info@halleonardeurope.com

In Australia contact:
Hal Leonard Australia Pty. Ltd.
4 Lentara Court
Cheltenham, Victoria, 3192 Australia
Email: info@halleonard.com.au

THE SINGER'S ANTHOLOGY OF GERSHWIN SONGS

Mezzo-Soprano/Belter

CONTENTS

Originally from:

Preface

The songs of George Gershwin are some of the best creations in "The Great American Songbook." Written most often in collaboration with his brother Ira as lyricist, these songs are loved around the world. There is good reason they have become timeless standards. For *The Singer's Anthology of Gershwin Songs* we have selectively chosen the most well-known songs that represent Gershwin's large output.

This edition does not attempt to be historically approached, because the style of performing many Gershwin songs has changed since they were written in the 1920s–30s. The editorial aims were to give the singer and pianist a reliable, practical edition that presents a song in a fairly straightforward manner, but adapted in some ways to be useful for singers of today. The songs have not been re-harmonized, as they would be in "creative" arrangements.

Some specific things globally addressed:

1. We usually removed the melody from the right hand of the piano part. Not doubling the melody in the piano gives the singer much more expressive freedom.

2. We sometimes created what could be called a "singer ending," depending on the song, allowing for a satisfying, singer-friendly conclusion, sometimes with suggested optional high notes.

3. The typical notation of swing beat now in use did not exist in Gershwin's era. In those days a dotted eighth was followed by a sixteenth note to indicate swing beat. We have modernized this notation. Swing beat is indicated at the top of the song, or at the refrain.

4. Dynamics and articulations in this edition are a combination of Gershwin's and editorial suggestion. The aim was always to create an edition that supports a singer above all, and to give the singer some options but also much freedom. Dynamics are not often in the vocal line, but in the piano part. Singers should look to the piano part for interpretative ideas regarding dynamics.

5. We retained the verse for every song. As far as form, for many songs we created a repeat that goes back to the "bridge" rather than to the top of the refrain. This, of course, is common practice in arrangements for singers.

6. If editorial changes were small or just a matter of taking the melody out of the piano part, songs are uncredited as to arranger/editor. If a song has more subjective arranging, the editor/arranger is credited.

Except for the selections from *Porgy and Bess* (not including "Summertime" for the Mezzo-Soprano/Belter, Tenor and Baritone volumes), songs are *not* in original keys. This is for practical vocal reasons. Original keys for songs written for musicals in the 1920s or 1930s don't mean much except for historical reasons. Those shows are not often performed today as musicals, so there is little reason for a singer to know the original key if cast to match the orchestral parts. Keys have been chosen to flatter a majority of singers of a particular voice type.

Soprano range for musical theatre is lower than for opera, as it is primarily middle voice singing, and keys were chosen for a typical soprano musical theatre head voice/chest voice mix. For Mezzo-Soprano/Belter, keys have been chosen that allow warmth in the voice, and straddle those who sing with a more classical sound with those who belt, or who sing with a belt/legit voice mix. Tenor keys are often a bit higher than soprano keys, but still contained. Baritone keys avoid too much constant low *tessitura* but keep the voice in a comfortable range.

The selections from *Porgy and Bess* appear here in their original form, without changes, except for transpositions in the case of "Summertime," a song recorded by thousands of female and male singers. Outside the opera, as a stand-alone song, it is certainly for anyone to sing. Though these volumes are overwhelmingly for solo voice, singers will certainly welcome having the duets "Bess, You Is My Woman" and "I Loves You Porgy" in the soprano and baritone volumes.

It would not best serve the singer of today to present every song as originally published, either from vocal scores of the shows or from original editions of sheet music. Performing traditions have changed. Some songs that were written as upbeat, rhythmic and carefree in style in the 1920s simply aren't performed that way anymore. Good examples are "Embraceable You" and "I've Got a Crush on You." These songs maintain Gershwin's harmonies, but have been edited and arranged to allow them to be ballads, as they have been commonly performed since at least the 1950s.

Well-established performing traditions since the important recordings of the 1950s inform how many of these songs are usually sung today. For the verse in quite a few songs, we created a basic accompaniment so that the singer can sing them freely, without strict rhythm and tempo. This approach was taken for "I've Got a Crush on You"; "Love Is Here to Stay"; "Love Walked In"; "The Man I Love"; "'S Wonderful"; "Somebody Loves Me"; "Someone to Watch Over Me"; "Soon"; "They All Laughed'; "They Can't Take That Away from Me" and "Who Cares?"

When in our opinion it heightened the impact of a song, we played with the form a bit. For example, in this edition of "Embraceable You" we began with the refrain, then present the verse, then a return to the refrain with a different treatment. In other songs, such as "A Foggy Day," we created sections of the refrain to be sung freely, simplifying the piano part, to give the singer the most opportunity for expression. There are other such examples.

Free vocal arranging, beyond suggested high notes, happens only in two songs, with written out suggested "improvisations" in "Blah, Blah, Blah" and "By Strauss."

Landmark recordings by Ella Fitzgerald, Frank Sinatra and other great singers of the standards era influenced this edition at times. We admit we stole Ella's nifty ending for "But Not for Me": "...and there's no knot, I guess he's [she's] not for me." Any singer getting to know Gershwin songs should listen to Ella Fitzgerald, Frank Sinatra, Michael Feinstein, Tony Bennett, Rosemary Clooney, and so many other great singers of standards.

Some songs as originally written had lyrics for both female and male singers, because they were sung in a form that traded verse/refrains between characters, typical of the 1920s. For this edition, we have chosen lyrics for the appropriate gender of the voice type volume. There are times in lyrics when "she" is changed to "he" for the women's volumes, or vice versa, and other such minor instances addressing gender, such as "his" and "her."

More than anything else, the Gershwin brothers gave the entire world a distinctly American, glamorous, casual and warm definition of romance in song. In performing Gershwin songs, don't make the mistake of doing them without awareness of the wit that is almost always present. In the best of urbane songs of the 1920s and 1930s by the Gershwins, Rodgers & Hart, Cole Porter, and a few others, it wasn't enough to say "I love you" in a love song. It was the style and the cleverness of how that was delivered, often with some self-deprecating humor.

This four-volume series was a team effort. Assistant editor/arrangers Joel Boyd, Brendan Fox and Joshua Parman played a vital role in bringing this to life, and I acknowledge their contributions with gratitude.

Richard Walters
Editor

George and Ira Gershwin

George Gershwin (1898–1937) was one of the first American composers to succeed in both popular song and classical genres, bringing the rhythmic drive, brashness, and swooning sounds of the Jazz Age into the concert hall. Born and raised in New York City, Gershwin found early work as a song plugger in Tin Pan Alley, where people flocked to hear live previews of new songs. As he continued playing and recording piano rolls, he also began to promote his own compositions. His first hit came in 1919 with "Swanee," which Al Jolson performed after hearing it at a party. Though Gershwin collaborated on several Broadway musicals with lyricists William Daly and Buddy DeSylva, he found his most successful and long-term creative partnership with his brother Ira (1896–1983). Beginning with the musical comedy *Lady, Be Good!* in 1924, the Gershwin brothers were an unstoppable force. Songs such as "Someone to Watch Over Me," "Summertime," "A Foggy Day," Embraceable You," "I Got Rhythm," "The Man I Love," and others are now considered some of the most beloved and enduring American standards, usually referred to as part of the Great American Songbook.

George Gershwin's groundbreaking concert works like *Rhapsody in Blue* (1924) and *Concerto in F* (1925) fused jazz style with classical instrumentation, and remain some of the most popular and widely performed American compositions of all time. The opera *Porgy and Bess* (1935), based on DuBose Heyward's novel and subsequently his own stage adaptation, was notable at its premiere for its all-black cast and musical melting pot of folk, jazz, and more traditional classical influences. The accessible, easily-excerptable musical numbers like "Summertime" and have surely helped its longevity.

George never married, though he had a ten-year affair with fellow composer Katherine "Kay" Swift. His life was tragically and suddenly cut short at age 38 by a malignant brain tumor. In the years after his death, Ira and Kay devoted much time to organizing, annotating and publishing George's work. After a three-year hiatus, Ira also continued to write songs, teaming up with composers including Harold Arlen, Jerome Kern, and Kurt Weill. His most notable work during this period was for the 1954 Judy Garland film *A Star Is Born*. Ira Gershwin died at age 86 in Beverly Hills, California.

Today, the Gershwins' musical legacy is preserved in the George and Ira Gershwin Collection in the Library of Congress. Two prestigious awards bear their namesake: the George and Ira Gershwin Lifetime Musical Achievement Award, issued by UCLA to such recipients as Frank Sinatra and Julie Andrews, and the Library of Congress Gershwin Prize for Popular Song.

BLAH, BLAH, BLAH

edited and arranged by
Richard Walters

Music and Lyrics by GEORGE GERSHWIN
and IRA GERSHWIN

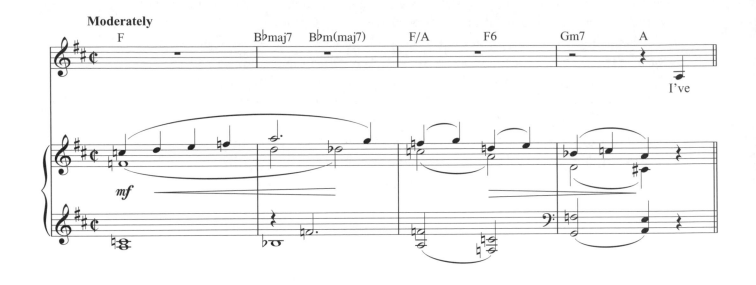

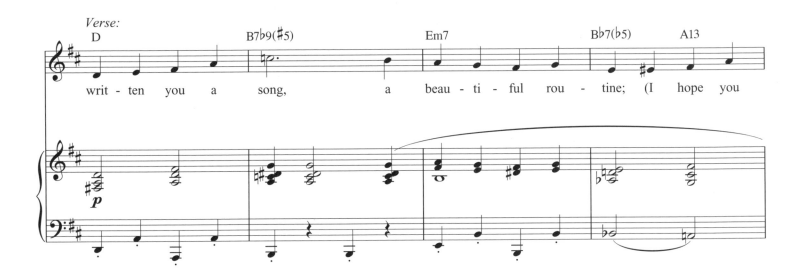

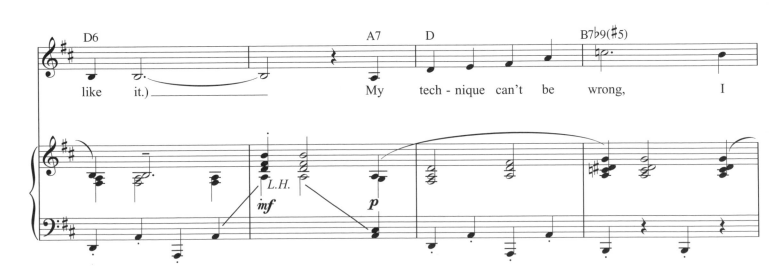

BUT NOT FOR ME

Music and Lyrics by GEORGE GERSHWIN
and IRA GERSHWIN

*On the repeat, the pianist might play R.H. 8va until **

10

BY STRAUSS

edited and arranged by
Richard Walters

Music and Lyrics by GEORGE GERSHWIN
and IRA GERSHWIN

*Sing this tune from "Tales from the Vienna Woods" on any improvised syllable.
This section is not original from Gershwin, but an editorial arrangement.

HOW LONG HAS THIS BEEN GOING ON?

edited and arranged by
Richard Walters

Music and Lyrics by GEORGE GERSHWIN
and IRA GERSHWIN

Verse:

'Neath the stars at ba - zaars of - ten I've had to ca - ress men.

Five or ten dol - lars then I'd col - lect from all those yes - men.

Don't be sad, I must add that they meant no more than chess - men.

EMBRACEABLE YOU

edited and arranged by
Richard Walters

Music and Lyrics by GEORGE GERSHWIN
and IRA GERSHWIN

FASCINATING RHYTHM

Music and Lyrics by GEORGE GERSHWIN
and IRA GERSHWIN

A FOGGY DAY (IN LONDON TOWN)

Music and Lyrics by GEORGE GERSHWIN
and IRA GERSHWIN

34

HE LOVES AND SHE LOVES

Music and Lyrics by GEORGE GERSHWIN
and IRA GERSHWIN

37

I GOT RHYTHM

Music and Lyrics by GEORGE GERSHWIN
and IRA GERSHWIN

I'LL BUILD A STAIRWAY TO PARADISE

Words by B.G. DeSYLVA
and IRA GERSHWIN
Music by GEORGE GERSHWIN

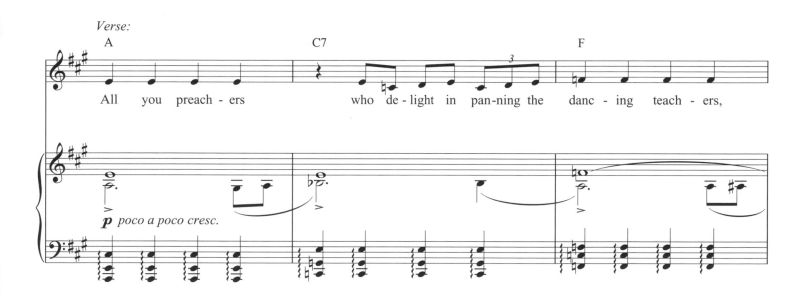

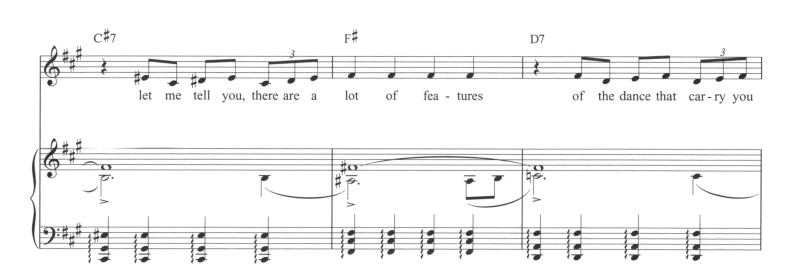

I'VE GOT A CRUSH ON YOU

Music and Lyrics by GEORGE GERSHWIN
and IRA GERSHWIN

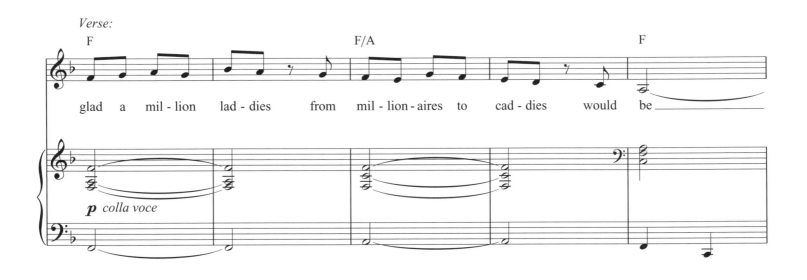

*On the repeat, the pianist might play the R.H. 8va until **.

ISN'T IT A PITY?

Music and Lyrics by GEORGE GERSHWIN
and IRA GERSHWIN

How well you planned it! I just could-n't stand it an - y - more!

Not fast, with expression
Refrain:

It's a fun - ny thing, I look at you,_ I get a thrill_

I nev-er knew._ Is - n't it a pit - y we nev-er met_ be -

fore? Here we are at last!

THE MAN I LOVE

edited and arranged by
Richard Walters

Music and Lyrics by GEORGE GERSHWIN
and IRA GERSHWIN

Andantino semplice

Somewhat freely
Verse:

When the mel - low moon be - gins to beam, ev - 'ry night I

dream a lit - tle dream; and of course Prince Charm-ing is the theme: the

he for me. Al - though I re - al - ize as well as you

62

LET'S CALL THE WHOLE THING OFF

Music and Lyrics by GEORGE GERSHWIN
and IRA GERSHWIN

LOVE IS HERE TO STAY

Music and Lyrics by GEORGE GERSHWIN
and IRA GERSHWIN

73

LOVE WALKED IN

Music and Lyrics by GEORGE GERSHWIN
and IRA GERSHWIN

Slowly, with much expression

Refrain:

Love walked right in and drove the shad-ows a - way.

Love walked right in and brought my sun - ni - est day.

One mag - ic mo - ment and my heart seemed to know

MAYBE

Music and Lyrics by GEORGE GERSHWIN
and IRA GERSHWIN

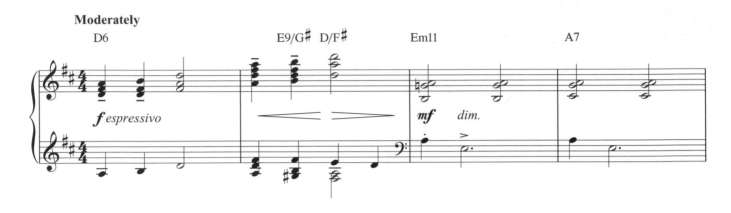

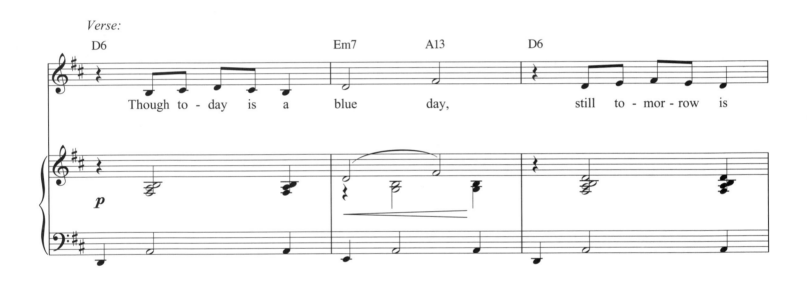

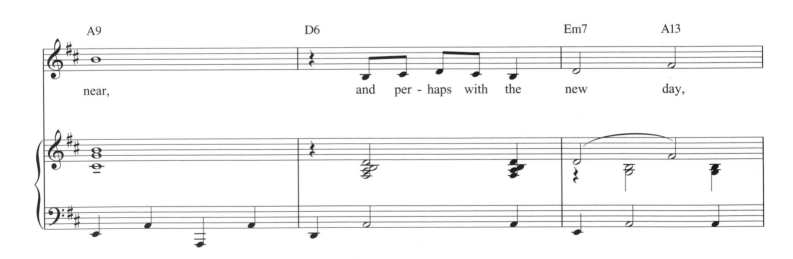

MY MAN'S GONE NOW
from *Porgy and Bess*

Music and Lyrics by GEORGE GERSHWIN,
DuBOSE and DOROTHY HEYWARD
and IRA GERSHWIN

Since I lose__ my man.

Ole Man Sor - row sit-tin' by de fire - place,

Ly - in' all night long____ by__ me in de bed.__

NICE WORK IF YOU CAN GET IT

Music and Lyrics by GEORGE GERSHWIN
and IRA GERSHWIN

SOMEONE TO WATCH OVER ME

Music and Lyrics by GEORGE GERSHWIN
and IRA GERSHWIN

'S WONDERFUL

Music and Lyrics by GEORGE GERSHWIN
and IRA GERSHWIN

Moderately, with gentle rhythm

Refrain:

1. 'S won - der - ful! _____ 'S mar - vel - ous! _____
2. 'S won - der - ful! _____ 'S mar - vel - ous! _____
3. 'S mag - ni - fique! _____ 'S what I seek! _____

SOMEBODY LOVES ME

Music by GEORGE GERSHWIN
Lyrics by B.G. DeSYLVA
and BALLARD MacDONALD

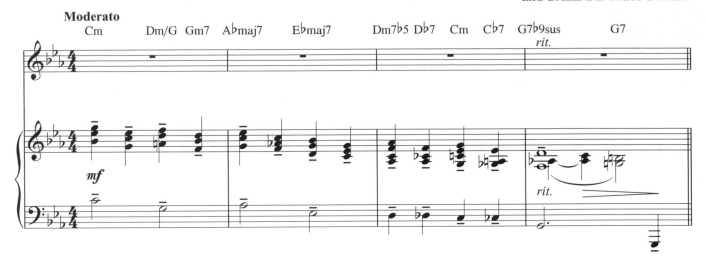

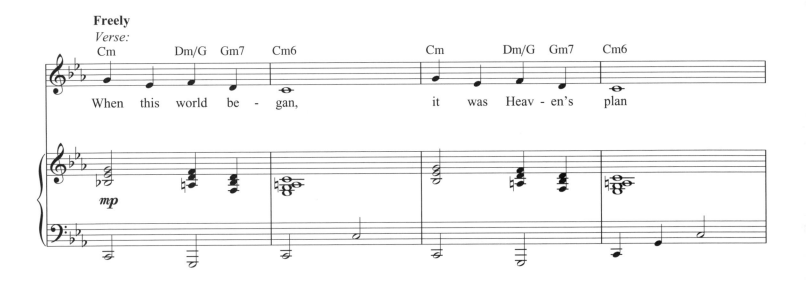

SOON

Music and Lyrics by GEORGE GERSHWIN
and IRA GERSHWIN

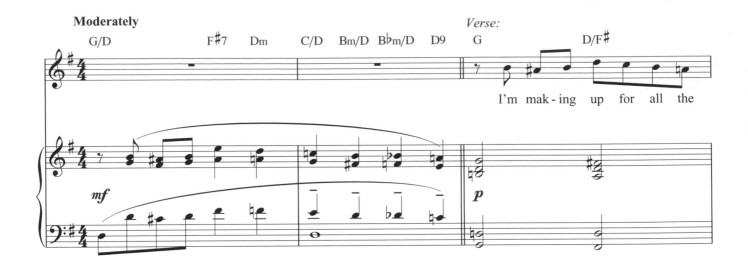

I'm mak-ing up for all the

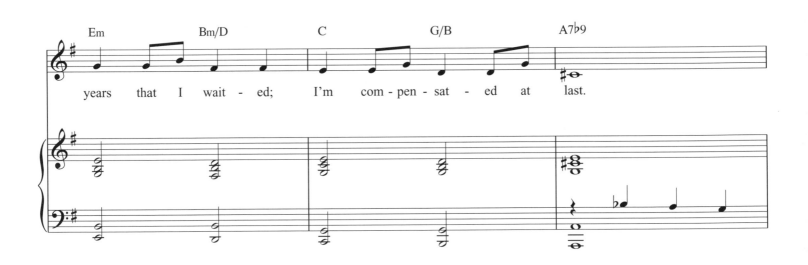

years that I wait - ed; I'm com-pen-sat - ed at last.

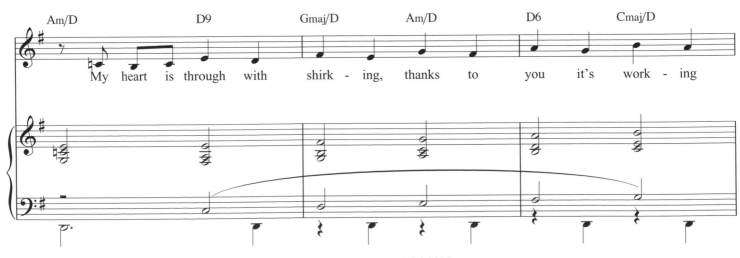

My heart is through with shirk - ing, thanks to you it's work - ing

SUMMERTIME
from *Porgy and Bess*®

Music and Lyrics by GEORGE GERSHWIN,
DuBOSE and DOROTHY HEYWARD
and IRA GERSHWIN

an' you'll take ___ the sky. _____ But till that

morn-in' ___ there's a noth-in' can harm you _____ With

Dad - dy an' Mam - my* stand - in' by. _____

opt. *mp*

mp

dim.

dim.

ten.

8va

*Some singers prefer to sing "mama".

THEY ALL LAUGHED

Music and Lyrics by GEORGE GERSHWIN
and IRA GERSHWIN

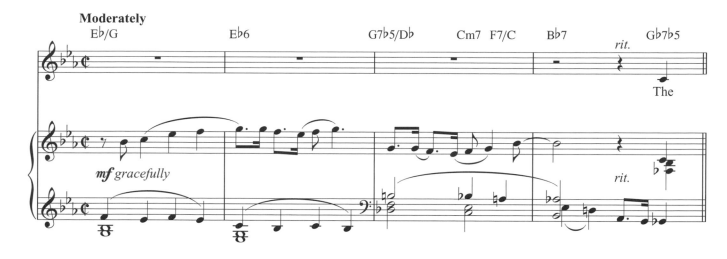

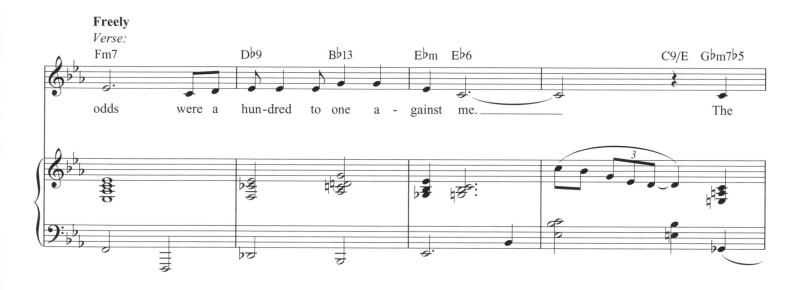

odds were a hun-dred to one a-gainst me. _____ The

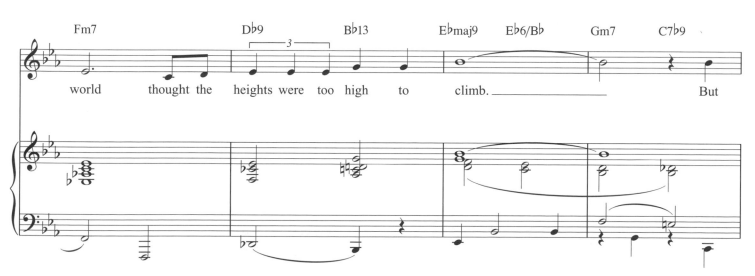

world thought the heights were too high to climb. _____ But

114

*Piano R.H. 8va 2nd time until **.

THEY CAN'T TAKE THAT AWAY FROM ME

Music and Lyrics by GEORGE GERSHWIN
and IRA GERSHWIN

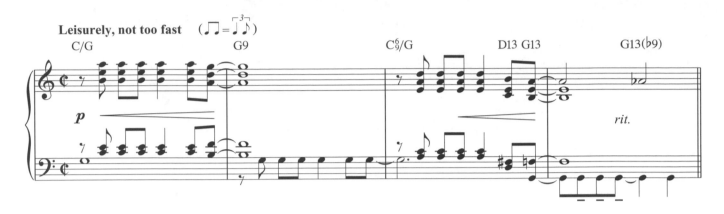

Freely; moving forward, speech-like

Verse:

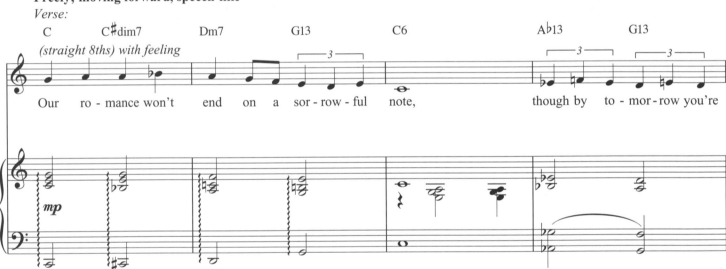

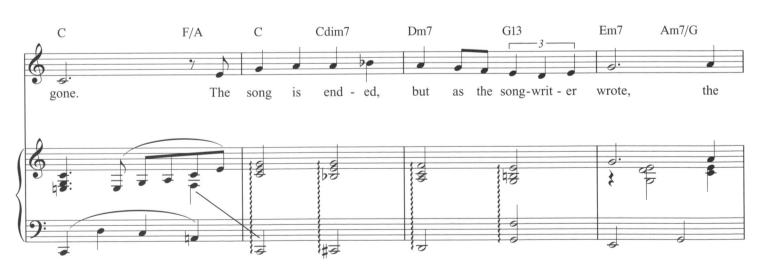

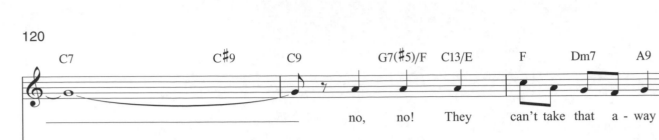

no, no! They can't take that a-way from me!

The way your smile just beams, ___ they way you sing off key, __

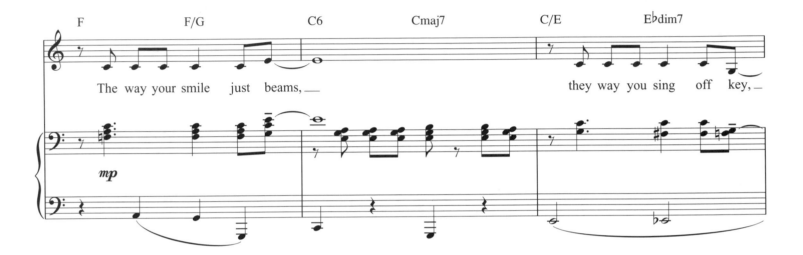

the way you haunt my dreams, ___

no, no! They can't take that a-way from me! __ We may

WHO CARES?
(So Long As You Care for Me)

Music and Lyrics by GEORGE GERSHWIN
and IRA GERSHWIN

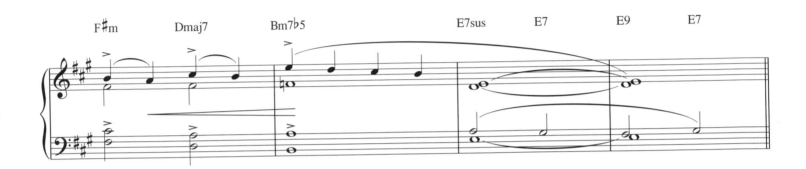